TIGERS in AFRICA

Published in South Africa under the
LLAREC Series in Visual History
Series editors: Pippa Skotnes and Martin Hall
Production and design editors: Jos Thorne and Pippa Skotnes

Design and typesetting by LLAREC
The Museum Workshop at the University of Cape Town

Published in South Africa by
    The University of Cape Town Press
    PO Box 24309
    Lansdowne 7779
    South Africa

    ISBN 1-919713-63-8

Published in Namibia by
    Out of Africa
    PO Box 21841
    Windhoek, Namibia

    ISBN 9916-2-231-4

Published in the United States of America by
    The University Press of Virginia
    PO Box 400318
    Charlottesville, VA 22904-4318
    USA

    ISBN 0-8139-2129-5

Library of Congress Cataloging-in-Publication Data is available from the Library of Congress.

Reproduction by Scan Shop

Printed and bound by Mills Litho, Cape Town.

Tigers in Africa

Stalking the Past at the Cape of Good Hope

CARMEL SCHRIRE

THIRD GLYNN ISAAC MEMORIAL LECTURE

CAPE TOWN 1999

Acknowledgements

Tigers in Africa: Stalking the past at the Cape of Good Hope is presented with the greatest affection to the family of Glynn Isaac. I thank my colleagues at the University of Cape Town, Martin Hall and John Parkington, for inviting its original presentation at the World Archaeological Congress 4 in Cape Town in 1999. I was honoured to attend the birthday celebrations for Nelson Mandela in 2000, and I thank Francis Wilson and Fikile Bam for the kindness in arranging this matter. Pippa Skotnes, Jos Thorne and Elliott Jordan were instrumental in the design and execution of the book. For financial assistance in travel and production costs, I thank the Department of Anthropology and the Center for Human Evolutionary Studies (CHES) at Rutgers, The State University of New Jersey. For titular inspiration, thanks to Robert Blumenschine.

Prologue

Tigers in Africa: Stalking the Past at the Cape of Good Hope is an amended version of the third in the series of Glynn Issac Memorial Lectures that commemorates the career of one of Africa's most celebrated archaeologists. Glynn Llewellyn Isaac (1937–1985) was born at the Cape and educated first at the University of Cape Town and then at Cambridge University. His research in Kenya at sites such as Olorgesaillie and Koobi Fora helped create and transform the field of modern palaeoanthropology.

The talk on which this book is based was delivered at the University of Cape Town in January 1999 at the World Archaeological Congress 4. The large audience included members of the Isaac family, old friends from his birthplace, teachers like Desmond Clark, and count-less colleagues from all parts of the world, all of whom came to hear me situated Glynn in the history and archaeology of the Cape of Good Hope. The book widens the scope of that original lecture and brings the question of tigers in Africa in full circle, from its postu-lation by prisoners on Robben Island, back to the very men who originally argued the case there.

1. Bengal tiger cub, Tygerberg Zoo, Cape.

The matter of tigers in Africa was hotly debated at the Cape of Good Hope some 35 years ago, not in universities and learned journals, but in the confines of the maximum security prison on Robben Island, where an inmate named Nelson Mandela later articulated the issue as follows:

One day at the quarry, we resumed our discussion of whether or not the tiger was native to Africa ... Masondo ... who had ... been a lecturer at Fort Hare ... was vehement in his assertions that no tigers had ever been found in Africa. The argument was going back and forth and the men had put down their picks and shovels in the heat of the argument. This attracted the attention of the warders, and they shouted at us to get back to work. But we were so absorbed in the argument that we ignored the warders ... we were ... charged with malingering and insubordination ... handcuffed and taken to isolation.

(Mandela 1994:379)

2. Nelson Mandela and Walter Sisulu, Robben Island, 1966.

You can tell right off that whatever else they might have been, the warders were unattuned to philosophy and ecology, because the issue of tigers in Africa relates powerfully to both spheres. First, the Robben Island argument opens up the whole matter of carnivore evolution, and second, it encodes a metaphor of caged tigers and their rightful heritage.

I am going to weave in and out of both issues, bounding from reality to metaphor, but anchored at all times by a rope that holds me to one of the greatest tigers of our profession, our friend and colleague Glynn Isaac, whose rueful grin comes to mind as he watches me zipping around the past here at the Cape of Good Hope.

3. Tiger prowls at Tygerberg Zoo.

Let's first dispose of the matter of actual tigers in Africa. The simple answer is that there were never any tigers in Africa. Tigers evolved some 30 million years ago during the mid-Tertiary, as part of the great radiation of felids that eventually gave rise to many divergent forms, including the genus *Panthera*, of which lions, leopards, jaguars, cheetahs, cougars and tigers, still survive today.

But unlike lions and leopards, tigers were never in Africa. Their fossil ancestors appear about 1.5 million years ago, centred on their historical range and spreading from the Caspian Sea north to Siberia, possibly even into the Americas and east across India and China, down into the island chain of Indonesia. But never, then or now, did they range in Africa (Anton & Turner 1997:73–4).

4. Two seventeenth century porcelain tigers from China, retrieved from the shipwreck of the *Oosterland* (1697) in Table Bay, Cape Town.

Why then did anyone ever wonder about their presence here at the Cape of Good Hope?

The quick answer is that early travellers' records, whether English, Dutch or Portuguese, are stuffed full of lions and tigers (Raven-Hart 1967).

Early colonists were certainly familiar with lions. Here at the Cape of Good Hope were mountains called 'Lion's Head' and 'Lion's Rump'. Although actual lions padded across these particular slopes, the mountains here drew their names from their shape, in much the same way as Lion Mountain that overlooks the old Dutch fort in Mauritius was certainly named for its looks rather than its denizens.

5. Lion's Head and Lion's Rump (Signal Hill), Cape Town.

6. Lion Mountain, Mauritius. The ruins of the old Dutch VOC fort lie on the shore below.

Early renditions of the mountain backdrop at the Cape of Good Hope were often misleading because the European artists who had seldom seen the Cape themselves generally worked off the rough sketches and widely varying descriptions by early travellers. One of the most spectacular misrepresentations is a panorama of towering pillars that dwarf the tiny Cape settlement below.

1. Mont du Diable
2. Mont de la Table
3. Mont du Lion

Vue du Cap de Bonne Esperance

4 Hopital
5 Habitation des Hotentots
6 Jardin de la Compagnie

7. An eighteenth century rendition of the Cape settlement whose fantastically exaggerated mountains contrast with the chillingly realistic gallows and torture wheel on the beach.

Much the same type of error attended on representations of animals. Early colonists at the Cape were familiar with tigers. The great trading Dutch East India Company or Verenigde Oostindische Compagnie (VOC) that settled here in 1652, had a network of forts and posts strung out down the African coast and across the Indian Ocean into Indonesia. From their headquarters in Java, at Batavia, with its Tiger's Canal or Tijgersgracht (Taylor 1983:181), down to its most remote outposts, Company men heard word of tigers and craved their striped pelts. But although they knew an actual tiger when they saw one, they also called spotted hyaenas, bush cats, and especially leopards, *tijger* and later *tier* (Stead 1987:528).

Peter Kolben, the eighteenth century traveller at the Cape whose alleged eyewitness account has often been challenged, was confused about spots and stripes. He claimed that the Tygerberg mountain just north of Cape Town, was spotted like a tiger (Kolben 1731:7 vs Mentzel 1944:29) and drew the actual spotted Cape *tier* to illustrate his point.

François Le Vaillant visited the Cape in 1781 and described his own heroism during what he called a tiger hunt there. Many illustrations appeared in various editions of his travels, including one of a striped animal (Kennedy 1976, L96), though Le Vaillant himself concluded that the particular victim he bagged was a panther that the Hottentots called a spotted lion because, as he noted, 'in this part of Africa, there are no tygers' (Le Vaillant 1790:75).

8. Kolben's animals at the Cape. The spotted tiger is No. 4, third down on left.

The only indisputable picture of a tiger in Africa is a sketch entitled 'Dexterity of the Hottentots'. It was published in a book in England in 1795. The author is at present unknown, but the general format of the sketch hints at inspiration from Le Vaillant's earlier account (1790). Unlike Le Vaillant's carnivore of 1790 whose markings are confined to its tail, the animal in 'Dexterity' is a full-blown Bengal tiger. Given that a striped beast such as this could never have been hunted at the Cape, 'Dexterity' presents a perfect example of just how mistaken an artist can be, when commissioned to draw Cape people and their 'tyger', sight unseen.

9. Le Vaillant confronts a 'tyger'.

10. 'Dexterity of the Hottentots': a true tiger in Africa.

7

11. A view of the Cape of Good Hope under British rule, 1831.

Once the British took the Cape in 1795 the matter of tigers was clarified. Whatever local burghers might call a carnivore, there were certainly no Cape tigers here as there were in India. No chilling growls from the dark woods, no flash of stripes in the grass, no menacing paw prints at the gate of the stockade.

Tyger! Tyger! burning bright
In the forests of the night,

wrote William Blake in 1794 (Abrams & Greenblatt 2000:54). Nowhere is his famous imagery better shown than in a set of aquatints published between 1805 and 1807 in *Oriental Field Sports*. The artist, Thomas Williamson, served with the Bengal European Regiment for 20 years (Archer & Lightbown 1984:67).

He was there when villagers who lived in fear of marauding tigers enlisted the British to help them win this ecological war by shooting the predators at every opportunity, a 'sport' that carried on well into the twentieth century (Corbett 1960).

In Williamson's luminous images, the Bengal tiger skulks secretly outside the corral and publicly kills a bullock before an audience inside the stockade. Hunted by armed men perched in howdahs atop elephants, the tiger bides his time. He waits in the long grass and then leaps out at his tormentors. He bursts out from the sea at armed spearmen on the wharf and finally sinks down in the tussocks, killed by a poisoned arrow. In life as in death, his burning stripes and scarlet tongue proclaim defiance of the villagers, their stock, and their colonial intruders.

12. The Bengal tiger prowls at the gate of the stockade.

Back in Cape Town the British showed the public the real thing: a stuffed tiger shot in Nagpur, India, by one Captain Hunter, was purchased in London around 1890 and placed on view in the South African Museum, where today it still woefully bestrides its own anatomised skull.

But seeing is not always believing, and retaining the modern Afrikaans *tier* to denote leopard has kept the question alive to this day. In the isolation of Robben Island, with no research library, no museum and no resident expert, the tattered Xhosa-English dictionary that translated *ingwe* as *tier*, gave rise to the argument that if there were an indigenous word for tiger, the actual animal must have been seen here in Africa, somewhere, sometime (Fikile Bam, personal communication). In a prison where conversations were often terse and where arguments had to be whispered, the question of tigers in Africa was a ball to dribble, bat and kick around for as long as it took.

In the grim fastness of Robben Island, afloat on a dark sea of apartheid, it could take forever.

13. The Bengal tiger leaps at the hunter in his howdah.

14. Tiger in the South African Museum, Cape Town.

The irony was that the Island was peopled with tigers who had earned their stripes in the apartheid jungle. There were other tigers outside on the mainland, on the barricades, in jails, some camouflaged in classrooms, others exiled abroad, but all descended from a long line of fighters, leaping at new ideas, urging for what was right and roaring defiance into the prevailing gloom to light up the future with new ideas and hope.

I am going to leave actual tigers for now to focus instead on some of the metaphorical tigers that informed the life and times of our friend and colleague, Glynn Isaac.

Let's start with a quick tour of the history and ecology of his original habitat.

II

Glynn Isaac was born at the Cape of Good Hope around 60 years ago. He grew up in a scientific and social world forged by millions of years of ancestral human occupation and three centuries of colonial rule as part of the Dutch and British Empires. He reached manhood, peering out from under the dark cloud of apartheid. He left later in despair, heading for an Africa further north, where his homesickness might be assuaged knowing that he was still on this continent and following the traditions learned at its remotest tip.

They were powerful traditions, forged by generations of Africans at the Cape of Good Hope.

The Isaacs lived in an Edwardian villa called The Athenaeum, where the Royal Society of South Africa, heir to the earlier South African Philosophical Society, held its meetings (Fransen & Cook 1980:99).

15. The Athenaeum, Newlands, Cape.

All around were sites of scientific discovery. Nearby stood the farmhouse where John Herschel peered through his telescope in the 1830s to map the stars of the southern hemisphere (Evans *et al.* 1969). On the slopes of the Devil's Peak, in the estate of the Great Imperialist Cecil John Rhodes, sprawled the University and Rhodes' home, Groote Schuur. Here he kept a package of gold beads and a stone bird that had been brought to him from Great Zimbabwe, a site that he insisted was originally the biblical Ophir, stronghold of a Phoenician Empire that flourished there before being overrun by ancestral Shona people (Hall 1984; Summers 1975:59). This justified what Rhodes thought to be his rightful heritage, earning him the accolade of his Queen and the loathing of every right-thinking person who witnessed the slaughter and oppression that was used to extract the gold and the diamonds of the native people.

The Isaac home stood on the banks of the Liesbeek River, where the first farms of the old Dutch East India Company once flourished on the pastures of the indigenous cattlemen. Beyond the river lay the sweep of the City Bowl. Out to sea stood Robben Island, close enough to serve as a pantry for the original Dutch settlement and far enough to seclude lepers, felons and political dissidents such as Nelson Mandela.

16. Rhodes' estate and the University of Cape Town.

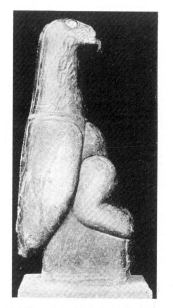

17. Soapstone bird, Great Zimbabwe.

13

Prospect des Vorgebürges der guten Hoffnung, abst dem Castell und Haafen, an der Spize von Afrika, ohnweit des Tafel-Löwen-und Teufels Berg.

Vuë du premontoir de bonne Esperance, avec le Port et chateaux au point d'Afrique, proche de la Montagne du table, du Lion et du Diable.

Gravé par J. Roth

18. Late eighteenth century view of the Cape, printed with the mountains in reverse.

14

19. Cape Town, 1988.

20. Castle of Good Hope, Cape Town, 1866.

On the original shores of Table Bay stood the old Castle. Here, in the glory days of the VOC, the Dutch Governor executed policy forged in Amsterdam and Batavia. From its storehouses crammed with food, cloth, Oriental porcelain and guns, he provisioned ships and bartered his way into the heartland of the continent, lubricating the acquisition of land and water with liquor, tobacco, beads and copper. Here, he imprisoned the enemies of the VOC, whether settler or native, as deaf to the banging of Company soldiers locked in the inky closeness of the Donkergat, or Black Hole, as he was to the soft clicks and entreaties of dispossessed cattlemen clustered around the Castle gates. Here too, the VOC tradition continued under British rule, with a Secretary's wife keeping a journal of daily life (Barnard 1994) and Zulu chiefs glaring out from their jail quarters on the great inner court (Thompson 1971:264).

Aspect du Fort

Montagne de la Table

Cap de bone Esperance

Fort

OCEAN MERIDIONAL

21. Fort de Goede Hoop at the Cape
settlement, 1668.

22. Soldiers' barracks near the Grand Parade, Cape Town, *c.* 1832–1835.

Alongside the Castle, atop the flattened remains of the original VOC fort, lay the Grand Parade.

23. City Hall, Cape Town, 1999.

Today a statue of King Edward VII gazes on the ornate City Hall (Picard 1969:114–15) where, on the day of his release in 1990, Nelson Mandela spoke to deafening cheers, and where a few years later, a vast groan greeted the loss of the Olympic bid.

More than two centuries earlier, Captain James Cook's men had camped on this expanse, enjoying the hospitality of what he called '... one great Inn fited [*sic*] up for the reception of all comers and goers ...' (Beaglehole 1974:266). In 1772, his artist William Hodges took a few steps back to paint one of the greatest renditions of sunlight on the mountains (Joppien & Smith 1985:11; Beaglehole 1974:309).

24. Table Mountain and Table Bay. W. Hodges, 1772.

Cook's first visit to the Cape in 1771 came at the end of a voyage to Tahiti to record the astronomical Transit of Venus, a matter addressed at the Cape by the famous team of Mason and Dixon. Cook's third voyage outbound, brought him here to scratch his initials on a window of the Colonial Bank in the middle of town (Bradlow 1970:20), and it might have brought him back again on the homebound stretch, except that he was slaughtered in the Hawaiian Islands, leaving to his successor the task of dropping off the gift of a mask from the natives of Nootka Sound in British Columbia (Beaglehole 1974:685–6).

Today it is one of the greatest treasures of the South African Museum (Summers 1975:3).

25. Nootka mask. South African Museum, Cape Town.

26. Chiappini Street, Bo Kaap, Cape Town.

If you stand on the Grand Parade today you can see the historical legacy of settlement that spreads way up towards the mountain slopes. Clustered on the side of Lion's Rump in Bo Kaap are the houses and mosques of former slaves from the East.

On the slopes of Devil's Peak lie the flattened remains of the old British District Six, a crowded enclave of people of colour that was brutally bulldozed during the apartheid regime. Straight ahead towards Table Mountain stands the old VOC slave lodge and the Company Gardens, where a long tradition of experimental and scientific horticulture preceded the botanical interests of Glynn Isaac's parents (Grove 1996:133–45).

27. District Six before the forced removals and destruction.
Gregoire Boonzaier, 1964.

Nearby stands the South African Museum crammed with collections that helped create the world's scientific history. Tiny fossils from Ceres in the Western Cape, that resemble those from Tasmania and the Falkland Islands, helped substantiate the theory of continental drift. Huge carnivorous reptiles from the Karoo illustrate the course of mammalian evolution and small lifelike Bushmen hunters speak to isolation and change (Fortey 1998:201; Summers 1975:201).

So much for a boyhood home. Now to some of the tigers who indirectly or clearly affected Glynn's world. I have chosen three cases: first, a pair of tigresses whose courage says something about the social history of the Cape; second, a scientist who knew a thing or two about slash and bite; and last, some of the tigers who taught Glynn more than they probably imagined.

28. South African Museum, Cape Town.

29. Below, left: *Uranocentrodon*, *c*. 225 million years old. South African Museum, Cape Town.
30. Below, right: *Erythrosuchus*, *c*. 200 million years old. South African Museum, Cape Town.

III

We here at the Cape of Good Hope belong to a Creole society forged over the past 500 years by indigenous people, colonists and slaves.

Until the British outlawed the trans-oceanic slave trade in 1807, slaves were brought to the Cape from trading networks all around the African coast and Madagascar, and from the Dutch trading empire in the East, where political dissidents who threatened the stability of the great Company were detained and later banished to this remote enclave.

Here many became known as the 'Cape Malays' (Davids 1980).

At its most picturesque, their Islamic legacy is encoded in the finely wrought detailing of eighteenth century Cape houses, carved and plastered by skilled Asian craftsmen, and in the dazzling gables of the wine route, fashioned by Huguenot vintners and their slaves.

31. Morgenster, a VOC period farm in the Western Cape.

It still echoes each day in the high nasal cries of muezzins that float across the city calling the faithful to prayer.

32. Longmarket Street, Bo Kaap, Cape Town.

It segues also, on occasion, into a sea of Muslim demonstrators swathed in anonymity.

33. PAGAD demonstration, Cape Town, 1998.

In the vast historiography of slavery, ours is but a minor variant. It lasted for less than 200 years as opposed to millennia in Europe and it involved the importation of a mere 63,000 people, as compared with millions in America and the Caribbean (Shell 1994:40).

But cliometrics seldom textures suffering. For that you need a story.

Slavery colours our history, architecture, politics and everyday life. Archaeologists reify slavery in a house, a slave lodge, a shackle, chain or whip. My tale arises from a museum artefact housed in the dim recesses of the Koopmans-De Wet House in Cape Town.

34. Koopmans-De Wet House, Cape Town.

35. Interior, Koopmans-De Wet House, Cape Town.

It is an elegantly wrought candelabrum, one of a pair made around 1790 by a Georgian craftsman in England. It forms part of a large collection purchased by the wealthy Cape settler family of Van Breda, after the abolition of slavery 150 years ago, with the compensation money they received from the British government for the loss of their slaves (Fransen & Cook 1980:59; Koopmans-De Wet House, 1988: 6 No. 6; South African Cultural History Museum catalogue 001–849, Nos 90a, b). It spells out the price of slavery every bit as explicitly as do the official regulations that valued 38,427 Cape slaves at an average of £73 apiece (Meltzer 1994:181) and it reflects in its quiet glow the life and times of two particular slaves, Antje and her daughter Martje, tigresses here at the Cape of Good Hope.

36. Candelabrum, Koopmans-De Wet House, Cape Town.

29

Her father, Muller, died in 1821 when the child was 12 years old (CAD CSC 2/1/1/6, No. 3(a): 9, No. 3(b)). He had never married Antje but had always vowed to leave a legacy to manumit and to support his child. Five years went by and nothing happened. Then fearing the worst, Antje filed a complaint that went to the Cape Supreme Court (CAD SO4/2:28). It turned out that Muller had left two wills. The first, dated 1816, did exactly what he had promised his daughter he would do (CAD CSC 2/1/1/6 No. 1). The second, dated 1819, left his entire estate to his settler relatives (CAD CSC 2/1/1/6, No. 2, MOOC 7/1/84).

The plaintiff's counsel argued that the will was inexplicable; that Muller had had no legal wife nor any other children, and that he had lived in concubinage with Martje's mother, Antje, the property of Mr Johannes Albertus van Breda, for some 15 years. Her owner testified that the pair had shared a strong and unchanged mutual affection which had still been powerful when he had died in the arms of the said Antje (CAD CSC 2/1/1/6, No. 3(a):12–13). However, the court upheld the last will leaving Martje, his daughter, a slave and the property of Mr Johannes Albertus van Breda of the farm De Hoop in the Table Valley.

The court record ends here. The *Register of Slaves* goes on to record the continuing servitude of both women, as well as the subsequent birth of two children to Martje, a daughter and son, all of whom were slaves of Mr van Breda (CAD SO6/14:329).

So here we have an open and shut case of a court upholding the last will and testament according to time honoured codes.

Why then include this mundane tale under a rubric of tigers in Africa?

37. A Cape slave woman and her children, *c.* 1800.

Antje van de Kaap was born here in about 1790 (CAD SO6/13:11). Aged 19, she had a daughter, Martje, with her lover, 22 year old Johan Christoffel Lodewyk Muller (CAD CSC 2/1/1/6, No. 3(a):7–8). He was a freeman, while Antje and their child Martje were slaves, and as such were the property of Mr Johannes Albertus van Breda of the farm De Hoop in the Table Valley (CAD SO6/13:11; SO6/14:329).

38. Cape Town, *c.* 1810, with sailors (left) and two slaves (right).

DE KAAP STAD
OF
TAFEL VALEY

39. Disposition of homesteads and farms in the Table Valley, *c.* 1804. The Van Breda estates lie on the upper slopes in centre field.

Let's start with the home of these slaves.

Stand at the Waterfront today and look up towards Table Mountain. Then run your eyes from the uppermost houses, down to where the slopes flatten out at the tower of the Gardens Centre. From 1731–1877, these were the estates of the Van Bredas.

32

40. Michiel van Breda, 'Laird of Oranje Zicht'.

Now to their owner: Johannes Albertus van Breda belonged to one of the richest families at the Cape. The founder, Pieter, immigrated from the Netherlands in 1720, and in 1731 he bought a farm on the slopes of Table Mountain, whose name, Oranjezicht, may have reflected its avenues of orange trees or its commanding view of the Oranje bastion of the old Dutch castle on the seashore (Pentacost 1992:25–7). Holding the water rights to the stream that gushed down the great cleft of the mountain, the Van Bredas became market gardeners. They also became the richest landowners in the Table Valley. When their water rights ran out there, they colonised the land over the eastern mountains and maintained their wealth under British rule as pioneers of the burgeoning wool market.

The head of the family in Martje's time was her master's brother, Michiel van Breda (1775–1847).

Nicknamed the 'Laird of Oranje Zicht' (Burrows 1952:111) his life straddled the dying days of the Dutch East India Company and the establishment of British rule after the turn of the century. Following the political tradition of his father, who had championed the cause of the *Kaapse Patriotte* for burgher rights under the VOC (Mienie 1968a), Michiel espoused home rule under the British flag. He protested the imposition of abolition from Westminster, but eventually yielded to reality and participated in the Legislative Assembly of the British-ruled Cape Colony from 1834–1837 (Burrows 1952:98; Mienie 1968b).

Where their income was concerned, the Van Bredas of the Table Valley were farmers. Pieter held the contract as purveyor to the booming naval establishment. He was said to have pulled out his cabbages, roots and all, to enhance their freshness on board ship (Pentacost 1992:30). Michiel, his son, was a man of the Enlightenment, heir to the tradition of scientific horticulture in the widening world of invention and discovery. On the terraced slopes laid out by his grandfather, he cultivated rare trees such as coffee, guava, loquat and grapefruit. He also cultivated the finer side of life. Inside his house, built by slaves, candles gleamed from wall sconces of Sheffield plate and porcelain rested on a sideboard carved by the famous Cape designer, Anton Anreith.

41. Belfry, Oranjezicht, Cape Town.

Following the custom of the Dutch in Batavia, a slave orchestra enlivened the dining room. Inside, the passing hours chimed from a clock depicting King David in the Garden of Eden. Outside, the work schedule tolled from a great bell cast in England in 1775 to memorialise his grandfather, Michiel van Breda (1722–1777).

Down the hill from Michiel's Oranjezicht was the farm De Hoop, property of his brother, Johannes Albertus, who lived there with his wife Elizabeth, their four children, and, at various times between 1816 and 1826, some 96 listed slaves. Most of these slaves were born locally, though some adults came from the African coast and Mozambique, or from further east, from Bengal, Batavia and Bugi. Many of the men were labourers, but some were hawkers, cooks, carpenters, wagon drivers, herdsmen and masons, as well as a coachman and a tailor. The women were servant maids, cooks, wet-nurses and laundresses. Among them were Antje and her daughter Martje, a mere two out of some 34,000 slaves living in the Cape Colony at the time (Bird 1822:69; CAD SO6/13:11, 103; SO6/14:329).

Scholars have argued that, unlike plantation slavery in the Caribbean and American South, Cape slaves, whether urban or rural, were deeply enmeshed in the family structure of their owners, with the Master acting the role of father to his slaves (Shell 1994).

But Martje's biological father was no Master: he was a townsman, a lover, even something of a dandy.

42. Bell from Oranjezicht, inscribed 'Michiel van Breda 12 Septr 1775'.

43. A slave woman in the kitchen, c. 1800.

35

The birthplace of Johan Christoffel Lodewyk Muller (1787–1821) is not recorded. Although he was listed in court papers as a man of 'the lower class of people' (CAD CSC 2/1/1/6 No. 3(a):6), his possessions, itemised on his death, included several changes of clothes, gold cuff-links, rings, silver buttons, brooches and buckles, to say nothing of seven walking sticks, five of which were embellished with silver. He also left a feather bed and fine linen (CAD MOOC 7/1/84: 609–11, 619–21). He was rich enough to buy his daughter's freedom but he chose not to manumit her or her mother in his lifetime. Worse, he broke his long-term promise to do so after he died.

Why did he do this? Who knows? What does matter is that it took courage for his daughter to appear in court, for at the time of the case Martje was only 17 years old. Years of intimacy of one sort or another had produced a Creole population in which it was hard to distinguish Cape-born slaves from settlers on outward appearance. Looks and 'race' were not paramount in the early years of the nineteenth century. Status was. Being free or unfree was what mattered. Martje might have had a happy life growing up on the lovely estate, helping in the kitchen and dancing to the band, but all this paled alongside the singular fact that she, like her mother, was a slave, and as such was the property of her master. Certainly she was entitled under the law to bring her case to court, but at that time it was a very new law and one administered in a very intimidating environment.

Martje lost her case. Of course she did. The last will and testament always supersedes prior ones. Martje remained enslaved, as did her mother and her two children, born before the period of apprenticeship and final abolition of 1838 (Worden 1994:117).

Martje and her family disappear from the record into the large, free underclass, who went on working at

44. The Freed Slave. He is believed to be carrying a 'General Order' for the abolition of slavery in one hand and a flower in the other.

the only jobs they knew, under a growing set of laws that restricted the free movement of the poor (Worden 1994). Some argue that slavery formed the bedrock of South African existence (Shell 1994). Certainly its heritage lingered and some visitors felt it everywhere. Anthony Trollope, visiting Cape Town 40 years after the abolition of slavery, saw that '... the stains, the apathy, the unprofitableness of slave labour still remains. It had a curse about it that fifty years have not been able to remove' (1973:79).

The case of Antje and Martje is but a tiny footnote to slave historiography at the Cape and you may well wonder why, given so many more bloody acts of slave resistance here – acts that include a particularly violent murder of a Master, Mistress and infant son on an adjacent Van Breda farm in 1760 (Cairns 1980) – I chose to detail this particular small, sad footnote. The answer is that unlike the blood lust that engenders a killing, Antje and Martje had that defiant quality of the tigress at bay. In a strongly patriarchal society where free women had property rights, slave women had nothing. Whatever help advisers, lawyers, even owners might have offered, these two stood alone when they fought it out in the court. Martje might have wondered about her own father as she polished the Master's silver, seeing his face reflected in her own sparking blue eyes. None of this mattered. What mattered was that she and her mother set a tigerish precedent by demanding their rights, here at the Cape of Good Hope, almost 200 years ago.

45. The Cape of Good Hope, 1812.

IV

So much for historical tigresses. We move on now to a tiger who brought the complex web of predators right to our own doorstep; a scientist whose research focused world attention on this country, drawing scholars to scrutinise the roots of humanity.

I am speaking of course, of Raymond Dart.

Dart was born in 1893 in Australia. In 1923 he came to South Africa to fill the chair of anatomy at the University of the Witwatersrand (Tobias 1997). South Africa held great promise for anthropology at that time. The scientific world was intent on tracing human ancestry, not only through the actual fossil record but also through isolated people who might still be 'living fossils'. John Lubbock's dogma that '... the van Diemaner [sic] and the South American are to the antiquary what the opossum and sloth are to the geologist' (1869:416) seems simplistic, even absurd today, but in its time and for some time thereafter, it engendered some of our most treasured records of indigenous folk, including the Bleek and Lloyd archive of Bushman language and lore (Deacon & Dowson 1996).

So there was Dart, classifying prehistoric and modern people according to a scheme that included Bush and Boskop types, when, in 1924, a tiny fossil skull from the limeworks at Taung came into his hands. Chipping away with his wife's knitting needle, he recognised it as a bipedal hominid ancestral to ourselves. He postulated it as a missing link between extinct and modern apes and man (Dart 1925). His conclusions challenged claimants for an Asian ancestry and flew in the face of the Great Chain of Command that insisted that the field be defined by Britain, not Johannesburg (Dubow 1995:42–7; Tobias 1992).

46. Raymond Dart and the Taung skull, c. 1925.

Much has been made of Dart's epiphany and its subsequent fire storm, but that is not at issue here. What I want to discuss is how Dart's vision of the life and times of early hominids like this set the stage for later work.

There were two sides to Dart's vision. The mild one held that when ancestral hominids came out of the trees they became gentle omnivores, adding fish, frogs, turtles, lizards, and maybe small buck, to a former vegetarian diet (1926:320–1; 1940:177–8). The violent one arose from his observation that the associated animal bones in caves such as Makapansgat in Northern Province, were broken in a way that reflected the hunting, killing and butchery of animals using bone clubs, daggers and blades (Dart 1957:87–9).

I doubt that the world would have flocked to see evidence of a gentle omnivore, but as it turned out, violence carried the day, sweeping an unexpected advocate into the field. American playwright, Robert Ardrey, came to Africa in 1955 to cover the Mau Mau uprising in Kenya. The vastness of the land astonished him. The lion's roar and the enormity of the night sky left him desolate. Friends advised him to visit Dart to check out the discoveries of the bedrock of human nature in Africa, and the rest became history.

47. Makapansgat, 1960, showing roof collapse following lime working.

Ardrey played Huxley to Dart's Darwin with tremendous effect, if only because he knew everyone who was anyone, anywhere. 'Dart', wrote Ardrey, 'was a genius' (1961:185). In Johannesburg, he held an australopithecine jaw and felt the death blow it sustained when the boy was murdered (*ibid*:187). 'Not in innocence, and not in Asia, was mankind born,' began and ended *African Genesis* (*ibid*:11,347). It promulgated Dart's message that violence lay at the root of human evolution. '*Australopithecus africanus* lies buried not in limey caves, but in my heart and in your heart, and in the black man's down the street. We are all Cain's children, all of us' (*ibid*:357).

Ardrey died here at the Cape, in Kalk Bay, leaving his papers to Rutgers University, where my colleagues Robin Fox and Lionel Tiger closely followed his work on the origins of violence. How totemism lingers!

In some way, it doesn't matter that Dart's thesis of ancestral violence was wrong. His reputation was founded on the discovery of the first australopithecine and his recognition of patterns in bone residues, poeticised and promulgated by Ardrey, formed the basis of crucial later work.

Dart's heirs today include Bob Brain, who pioneered the field of cave taphonomy. He studied how living carnivores such as hyaenas, leopards, dogs and porcupines (but not, of course, tigers) kill and consume their prey. He then compared the broken bones they left behind with those found in limestone caves, in order to say whether they were the leavings of extinct carnivores or those of ancient human ancestors (Brain 1958, 1981, 1993). Other scientists set the evolution of australopithecines in a broad ecological context (Vrba 1996), experimented with burned bones to rule out the use of fire by early hominids (Brain & Sillen 1988) and more recently, studied bone chemistry to recognise the isotopic signature of different animals and to situate early hominids in the ancient food web (Lee-Thorp *et al.* 1994; Sponheimer & Lee-Thorp 1999).

48. The Bengal tiger in consumption mode.

49. A. J. H. Goodwin, *c.* 1930.

All of this work focused world attention on South African paleoanthropology. In his wonderful volume on Swartkrans, Bob Brain features a rogues' gallery of visitors: Lewis Binford, Alan Mann, Clark Howell, Desmond Clark, Don Johanssen, and of course, Glynn and Barbara Isaac (Brain 1993:14). Even the famous essayist, Bruce Chatwin, took time off from whisking around Europe in a train with Stuart Piggott, and letting Somerset Maugham play with his hair, to come to the limestone cave of Swartkrans and see where early man lived and died (Brain 1993:18; Clapp 1997:84). Today, Dart's baby, and others like him, fall into his gentler category as omnivorous bipeds, vulnerable enough to be caught, eaten and gnawed over by carnivores, but resourceful enough to provision themselves over long stretches of evolutionary time.

Dart's revolutionary findings were fresh and clear when Glynn Isaac began his studies at the University of Cape Town in the 1950s. Africa was the place to be for human origin studies. The field would soon be widened for comparison with finds at Olduvai Gorge and integrated into the framework of southern African prehistory articulated by Glynn's teacher, John Goodwin.

Goodwin was born in Pietermaritzburg in 1900 and studied at Cambridge, where he graduated in 1922. He returned to the University of Cape Town as the only qualified archaeologist in the country. In 1928, Goodwin proudly took his Cambridge teacher, Miles Burkitt, on a grand tour of southern African prehistory, only to realise at the end of the trip that Burkitt planned to publish as his own, everything he had been shown (Burkitt 1928; Goodwin 1958:32; Schrire *et al.* 1986:123; Shaw 1991). Goodwin took it on the chin. With tigerish speed he published a master sequence of the South African Stone Age, which rejected Burkitt's notion that this was a mere prehistoric cul de sac receiving all its past from the north (Goodwin & Van Riet Lowe 1929). Working almost single-handedly, he remedied the lack of sequences with extensive excavations of deep deposits at stratified caves such as Oakhurst (Goodwin 1938a, b, c), and finally, he set up an infrastructure in 1945, by founding the South African Archaeological Society and its journal, the *South African Archaeological Bulletin* (Deacon 1989).

Goodwin's vision of the field was deeply pragmatic. It incorporated the findings of geology, zoology and climatology, as well as the ethnoarchaeological link with living foragers, to contextualise material remains. Deduction was the keystone of his approach; a sensible figuring out of things that would later conform exceedingly well with the positivistic message of the New Archaeology. Glynn, in turn, drew on this strong empirical tradition in his subsequent studies in Cambridge. Here, Dorothy Garrod's monumental excavations in Palestine revealed a shift from Neanderthals to modern humans that was interpreted as pinpointing the origin of the Upper Palaeolithic occupation of Europe. Charles McBurney expanded her findings with his work in North Africa. Grahame Clark pioneered the economy of prehistoric Europe, and Eric Higgs showed that prehistoric animal predation reflected not only human technology, but also constraints of climate and range (Clark 1989).

Glynn absorbed all this, batting it around with his brilliant friend, David Clark, but mostly he followed the teachings of Charles McBurney. A decade later he penned his prize-winning essay in response to Jacquetta Hawkes' attack on what she saw to be McBurney's scientism (Hawkes 1968; Isaac 1971). Hawkes had recoiled with horror at McBurney's enumeration, fearful that 'science' would eviscerate the human past. It was just as well that Hawkes never addressed David Clarke's work, because if McBurney's 250 tables and graphs at £12 each stunned her, Clarke's use of systems analysis and numerical taxonomy would have dealt a *coup de grace*! Although Glynn's response never actually mentions McBurney, his prompt response to the attack betrays an abiding respect for his teacher, and perhaps something more. I think that McBurney's sweeping vision of prehistoric events instilled in Glynn a vein of romance, in the strict sense of the word, which deeply informed the thrust of his later work.

Romance, you ask? McBurney and romance? Let's see.

50. Charles McBurney (far right) and field crew, 1960.

51. Charles McBurney, detail.

American-born, Charles Brian Montagu McBurney was educated not on a family estate nor in major public schools, but by private tutors in a series of posh hotels in London and Europe (Clark & Wilkenson 1986). His eccentricity might have been temporarily muted by a degree at Cambridge, but it rebounded after his war service in the western desert, in a series of expeditions between 1947–1955 that culminated in his excavations in Libya at the great cave of Haua Fteah (McBurney & Hey 1955; McBurney 1967).

Romance is the last thing that might have sprung to mind seeing or reading McBurney. He was dark, thin, with a clipped English accent and delivered his opinions in a high-pitched squeak. His archaeology was crammed with graphs and tables, which he used to portray himself as an utterly objective researcher, comparing prehistoric cultural change to the mutations in a cultural organism (1967:14). Although he included something about pastoral nomads in his early Libyan work, he later held that history and the behaviour of living peoples had nothing whatsoever to say about long-term cultural change (*ibid*:15). I suggest that McBurney's protestations might have been a deliberate effort to cloak his adventurous romanticism. After all, as a young man, he had espoused one of the most romantic causes of our time, when he went to France during the Spanish Civil War to set up a hospital for men wounded in what many felt was the earliest clarion call against fascism (Paul Sinclair 1999, personal communication). Likewise, although his desert work may have seemed dry, it actually emanated from a long tradition of highly romantic archaeological research.

To explain: McBurney's Libyan work was the first post-war follow-up to the international expeditions in the 1930s. This was the high road to adventure and romance, travelled by luminaries such as Orde Wingate, saboteur of the Burmese supply lines, who was later dubbed 'Lawrence of Judea' for his part in the establishment of the State of Israel (Wingate 1934). Explorers combed the great sand sea of Libya, following the legends of Herodotus in search of the lost army of Cambyses and the oasis of Zezura. Wingate scooped up stone artefacts and potsherds from his perch on the hump of a camel, and another explorer, Count Laslo d'Almàsy, discovered rock paintings showing swimmers in a long-lost lake (Bermann 1934:463).

Was this the embodiment of Herodotus' legend? Archaeologist Gertrude Caton-Thompson decried their romantic interpretations of a lost oasis, saying 'I am an archaeologist and archaeologists deal with specimens and not with theories' (in Bermann 1934:466), but her caution did not deter a later author, Michael Ondaatje, from casting their adventures into *The English Patient*, one of the great romantic novels of our time (1992).

True, Ondaatje's hero, Count Ladislaus d'Almàsy, was no romantic. His writing was as dry as sand; his politics were unpleasantly pro-Nazi; he was no lover, and he was certainly no one's patient (Bermann 1934:469). Nevertheless, the setting of this work was so evocative, its quest so poignant, that the movie of *The English Patient* invites today's public to watch archaeologists in the dune fields, promising, 'Own the video now ... stay in love forever!'

52. Count Laslo d'Almàsy, rear, Libya, 1934.

44

A similar vein of archaeological romance ran deep in Glynn's teacher, there in the dunes and caves of Libya, and it ran deep in Glynn. When I first saw him in Cambridge in about 1961, he had just got back from a season with Eric Higgs in Libya. He wasn't merely rhapsodising about the desert, he was actually wearing Arab robes. Of course, it might just have been that his regular clothes were in the wash, but in an England still aswoon over the lighter side of Lawrence of Arabia, it evoked something more. Glynn's subsequent explorations of the plains of East Africa and the lake shores of the Great Rift Valley would follow the tempo of the Libyan quests. His culminating insistence that division of labour, transport, speech, and sharing life in home bases was rooted in our deep evolutionary past, encodes a deep romantic conviction that being fed, protected, nurtured, spoken to and cared for in a secure home, is the bedrock of human existence. The fact that he later specifically acknowledged McBurney – the man who wrote that history and living people tell us nothing about the past – for teaching him to think about early artefacts in a broad behavioural context, speaks powerfully to my interpretation (Isaac 1986:441).

Nowhere is Glynn's romanticism better illustrated than in a photograph snapped in the late 1950s in Cape Town.

It shows him and his twin brother, Rhys, in a University of Cape Town pageant called the 'Varsity Rag'. They are disguised as Charles Darwin and the Original Species. The question is, who's who? Surely one might assume that the budding scientist, Glynn, would play Darwin to the budding historian's Early Man. But that is not so. Instead, Rhys plays Darwin, to Glynn's role as the most romantic political conceptions of all time – that image birthed by the French Revolution – the Original Species of humankind and its spawn, the Noble Savage.

53. Glynn (right) and Rhys Isaac at the Varsity Rag, Cape Town, c. 1957.

45

Once he had left Cape Town and his Alma Mater, Glynn never returned to work in South Africa. Whether his work was charged with a romantic vision or not, he certainly never romanticised his excuses. He was quite blunt about it when he came to speak at a conference in Cape Town in 1979. He acknowledged the intellectual inspiration of his boyhood home and said openly that although tigers such as Goodwin and Dart had started him off, he could not bear to live out the legacy of tigeresses like Antje and Martje. Glynn turned his back on the politics of apartheid and its legacy of pain, wrought so patently in the caging of tigers such as Nelson Mandela.

His absence was our loss. Standing here where it all began, I know that Glynn would have been glad to know how debates about tigers kept men's minds alive on Robben Island. He would have rejoiced in the outcome of the New South Africa, with its deep legacy of tigers who shaped our history, tigers who taught him, and indeed, tigers like him, who continue to inspire the life and times of people here at the remotest tip of Africa.

54. The dying tiger.

55. The tiger at bay

Epilogue

There remains a final sting in the tale of tigers in Africa.

I was first drawn to the issue on reading the argument that had raged on Robben Island, and although I realised that the men there had based their claims on a point of linguistics, I also recalled that I had once seen a tiger-like creature in the historical iconography of the Cape. My mother, Sylvia, an avid collector of early views of the Cape, joined me in a search for this image. Together we trawled through the catalogues of collections (Kennedy 1967; 1975; 1976) scrutinising every image of a wild carnivore for a hint of stripes. To no effect: not a single tiger presented itself. Then finally, three years later, I unearthed a forgotten folio of prints in my own house in Princeton, New Jersey, and rediscovered the long-lost image in a print that I had probably bought years before in a street market in London or New York. Tantalisingly entitled 'The Dexterity of the Hottentots', it features some classically poised people, startled by an unmistakable Asian tiger. Now, armed with the title, date, and the names of the draftsman and engraver, I returned to the catalogues to identify its source. Again, no luck: numerous experts in universities and auction houses were equally baffled. The source of this 1795 print, clearly eased out of the pages of a book, remains unknown.

For all this, my joy at finding a Georgian rendition of an Asian tiger in Africa remained undimmed. At dinner in Princeton, I poured out the story to Francis Wilson who was on leave at Princeton University. Francis, son of my former teacher, Monica Wilson, had been a student with both Glynn and me at the University of Cape Town in the late 1950s. He was thoroughly conversant with the Robben Island debate, as he was with certain of its proponents.

He wasted no time.

'You must give it to Mandela,' he announced. 'What's more,' he added, 'you must give it to Madiba for his 82nd birthday.' He used Mandela's clan name as a mark of affection. 'Which is ...' frowning over his diary, 'on the 18th of July. He shares it with Fiks Bam. You know Fiks? Well, when they were all on Robben Island, they all used to be given those ghastly chocolate biscuits, those Romany Creams, for Christmas, and Mandela would save his to give to Fiks on their birthday.' He stopped, tightened his mouth, and added, 'Fiks will arrange it all!'

DEXTERITY of the HOTTENTOTS
Publifh'd Oct.ʳ 1.1795 by I.Wheble, Warwick Court London.

Newton delin.   Scott sculp.ᵗ

56. The tiger in Africa.

On the 18th July, I gift-wrapped a framed picture of 'The Dexterity of the Hottentots', and together with a box of Romany Creams and a copy of my book (Schrire 1995), caught an early flight from Cape Town to Johannesburg to meet the legendary Fiks. Mr Justice Fikile Charles Bam, now President of the Land Claims Court, had been a student along with Glynn, Francis and me at the University of Cape Town, and he and I had been classmates there in Monica Wilson's course, Social Anthropology II. On graduating, Fiks stood poised on the verge of a glowing career, only to be summarily incarcerated on Robben Island for ten years.

He taught anthropology in the quarry, and in the prison quarters that he shared with Nelson Mandela and Walter Sisulu, he learned to envisage the new South Africa.

He also engaged in arguments about tigers in Africa.

Forty years on, Fiks Bam seemed unchanged. Tall, handsome, and with the same wide smile of our student days, he drove to Madiba's home in Houghton, cruising smoothly and deliberately through every Stop sign, in the well-honed defensive strategy of the seasoned Gauteng resident.

He spoke gently, orchestrating the visit with diplomatic resolve:

'When we get there, put the presents on the side. Say hello, chat, listen, but wait till I talk about Romany Creams. Then you can talk about tigers'.

Madiba's home shone with Highveld sunshine sparkling off bevelled glass doors and with an abundance of good will. He got up from his chair to greet us, wishing Fiks the best of birthdays. His wife, Graça Machel, a stateswoman in her own right and currently Chancellor of the University of Cape Town, rose in her stylish ochre suit to greet us with kisses on both cheeks. Talk ran from this birthday, to previous ones, and on to the Robben Island days when Mandela and Bam had provided free legal aid to white warders to help them file their divorce papers. It hopped from oil-slicked Island penguins to township schools, and segued into a righteous indignation that certain people would rather track the route of sea birds back to their roosts, than of school kids to a square meal.

57. Nelson Mandela inspects the tiger in Africa in 'The Dexterity of the Hottentots'. Johannesburg, 2000.

It was a family affair, this birthday lunch. Grandchildren and even a great-grandchild came to kiss Madiba and wish him well. His wife sat at his right hand, tempting him to sample a selection of spicy foods that were set out on the immaculate white tablecloth in a long line. Kisses again when Chris Hani's widow appeared, her small features as still as steel. Then, as Walter Sisulu entered on the arm of a strong aide, it was time to renew the matter of tigers in Africa.

58. Discussing tigers in Africa. From left to right: Nelson Mandela, Walter Sisulu, Fikile Bam and Carmel Schrire. Johannesburg, 2000.

59. The tiger attacks from the sea.

First Fiks raised the subject of Romany Creams, which Mandela greeted with a knowing smile. Then we presented a copy of my book, and lastly, the picture. Fiks unwrapped it, speaking rapidly about tigers and *tiers* and *ingwe*. On the prearranged signal, I rose and spoke of tigers and artists, and of mistakes and metaphors.

I kept it short. Everyone smiled, but the nods emanating from certain quarters made me feel that this old picture might have confirmed certain old misapprehensions. Sisulu's contented expression made me wonder if I had muddied the matter for good!

But the kindness and smiles overrode it all, and soon we were shaking hands and wishing well again and leaving, while behind us, the well-wishers kept coming to the gate as the party went on.

Back at his office, Fiks called Francis Wilson. Their exuberant Xhosa greeting was followed by a courteous return to English as Fiks summarised the visit, the gift, the pleasure of it all. I heard Francis' laughter down the line and the smile wreathing Fiks' face confirmed the joy, the sheer, mindless, uninhibited joy that came from transforming a collector's passion and an academic concern, into a historic event.

Glynn would have loved it!

60. Tiger.

Bibliography

Abrams, M. H. & S. Greenblatt. 2000. *The Norton anthology of English literature*. Seventh edn. Vol. 2. New York: W. W. Norton & Company.

Anton, M. & A. Turner. 1997. *The big cats and their fossil relatives: An illustrated guide to their evolution and natural history*. New York: Columbia University Press.

Archer, M. & R. Lightbown. 1984. *India observed. India as viewed by British artists 1760–1860*. New York: Alpine Fine Arts Collection, Ltd.

Ardrey, R. 1961. *African genesis: A personal investigation into the animal origins and nature of man*. London: Collins.

Barnard, Lady Anne. 1994. *The Cape journals of Lady Anne Barnard 1797–1798*. A. M. Lewin Robinson, M. Lenta & D. Driver, (eds). Cape Town: Van Riebeeck II:24.

Bent, J. T. 1892. *The ruined cities of Mashonaland*. London: Longmans, Green & Co.

Beaglehole, J. C. 1974. *The life of Captain James Cook*. Stanford: Stanford University Press.

Bermann, R. A. 1934. Historic problems of the Libyan desert. *The Geographic Journal*, LXXXIII:456–63.

Bird, W. 1822. *State of the Cape of Good Hope in 1822*. Cape Town: C. Struik (Pty.) Ltd. Facsimile reprint (1966).

Bradlow, E. 1970. Travels of Captain Cook. *South African Panorama* 15, 11:20–3.

Brain, C. K. 1958. The Transvaal ape-man bearing cave deposits. *Transvaal Museum Memoir* 11. Pretoria: Transvaal Museum.

Brain, C. K. 1981. *The hunters or the hunted? An introduction to African cave taphonomy*. Chicago: University of Chicago Press.

Brain, C. K. 1993. Swartkrans: A cave's chronicle of early man. *Transvaal Museum Monograph* 8. Pretoria: Transvaal Museum.

Brain, C. K. and A. Sillen. 1988. Evidence from Swartkrans cave for the earliest use of fire. *Nature* 336:464–6.

Burkitt, M. C. 1928. *South Africa's past in stone and paint*. Cambridge: Cambridge University Press.

Burrows, E. H. 1952. *Overberg outspan: A chronicle of people and places in the south western districts of the Cape*. Cape Town: Maskew Miller Ltd.

Cairns, M. 1980. The Smuts family murders – 14.7.1760. *Cabo* 12:13–16.

Clapp, S. 1997. *With Chatwin: Portrait of a writer*. New York: Alfred A. Knopf.

Clark, G. 1989. *Prehistory at Cambridge and beyond*. Cambridge: Cambridge University Press.

Clark, J. D. & L. P. Wilkenson. 1986. Charles Brian Montagu McBurney (1914–1979): An appreciation. In G. N. Bailey & P. Callow (eds), *Stone-age prehistory: Studies in memory of Charles McBurney*: 7–25. Cambridge: Cambridge University Press.

Corbett, J. 1960. *Man-eaters of Kumaon and the temple tiger*. London: Oxford University Press.

Dart, R. A. 1925. Australopithecus africanus: The man-ape of South Africa. *Nature* 115:195–9.

Dart, R. A. 1926. Taungs and its significance. *Natural History* XXVI:315–27.

Dart, R. A. 1940. The status of Australopithecus. *American Journal of Physical Anthropology* 26:167–86.

Dart, R. A. 1957. The osteodontokeratic culture of Australopithecus prometheus. *Transvaal Museum memoir* 10. Pretoria: Transvaal Museum.

Davids, A. 1980. *The mosques of Bo-Kaap: A social history of Islam at the Cape*. Athlone: South African Institute of Arabic and Islamic Research.

Deacon, J. 1989. Introducing Goodwin's legacy. *South African Archaeological Bulletin Goodwin Series* 6:3–5.

Deacon, J. & T. A. Dowson. 1996 (eds). *Voices from the past: /Xam Bushmen and the Bleek and Lloyd collection*. Johannesburg: Witwatersrand University Press.

Dubow, S. 1995. *Scientific racism in modern South Africa*. Johannesburg: Witwatersrand University Press.

Evans, D. S., T. J. Deeming, B. H. Evans & S. Goldfarb (eds). 1969. *Herschel at the Cape. Diaries and correspondence of Sir John Herschel, 1834–1838*. Austin and London: University of Texas Press.

Fairbridge, D. 1924. *Lady Anne Barnard at the Cape of Good Hope, 1797–1802*. Oxford: The Clarendon Press.

Fortey, R. 1998. *Life: A natural history of the first four billion years of life on earth*. New York: Alfred A. Knopf.

Fransen, H. & M. A. Cook. 1980. *The old buildings of the Cape*. Cape Town: A. A. Balkema.

Goodwin, A. J. H. 1938a. Archaeology of the Oakhurst shelter, George. *Transactions of the Royal Society of South Africa*, XXV:229–45.

Goodwin, A. J. H. 1938b. Archaeology of the Oakhurst shelter, George. *Transactions of the Royal Society of South Africa*, XXV:247–58.

Goodwin, A. J. H. 1938c. Archaeology of the Oakhurst shelter, George. *Transactions of the Royal Society of South Africa*, XXV: 303–24.

Goodwin, A. J. H. 1958. Formative years of our prehistoric terminology. *South African Archaeological Bulletin*, XIII:25–33.

Goodwin, A. J. H. & C. van Riet Lowe. 1929. The Stone Age Cultures of South Africa. *Annals of the South African Museum*, 27:1–289.

Grove, R. H. 1996. *Green imperialism: Colonial expansion , tropical island Edens, and the origins of environmentalism, 1600–1860*. Cambridge: Cambridge University Press.

Hall, M. 1984. The burden of tribalism: The social context of southern African Iron Age studies. *American Antiquity* 49: 455–67.

Hawkes, J. 1968. The proper study of mankind. *Antiquity* 42: 255–62.

Isaac, G. L. 1971. Whither archaeology? *Antiquity* 45:123–9.

Isaac, G. L. 1986. Foundation stones: Early artefacts as indicators of activities and abilities. In G. N. Bailey & P. Callow (eds), *Stone Age Prehistory: Studies in memory of Charles McBurney*: 221–41. Cambridge: Cambridge University Press.

Joppien, R. & B. Smith. 1985. *The art of Captain Cook's voyages. 2. The voyage of the* Resolution *and* Adventure *1772–1775*. New Haven: Yale University Press.

Kennedy, R. F. 1967. *Catalogue of pictures in the Africana Museum*. 3, E–L. Johannesburg: Africana Museum.

Kennedy, R. F. 1975. *Catalogue of prints in the Africana Museum*. 1, A–K. Johannesburg: Africana Museum.

Kennedy, R. F. 1976. *Catalogue of prints in the Africana Museum*. 2, L–Z. Johannesburg: Africana Museum.

Klose, J. 1994. Excavated Oriental ceramics from the Cape of Good Hope: 1630–1830. *Transactions of the Oriental Ceramic Society* 57:69–81.

Kolben, P. 1731. *The present state of the Cape of Good-Hope: or, A particular account of several nations of the Hottentots*. 2. London: W. Innys.

Koopmans-De Wet House. 1988. *Catalogue*. Cape Town: Creda.

Lee-Thorp, J. A., N. J. Van der Merwe, & C. K. Brain. 1994. Diet of *Australopithecus robustus* at Swartkrans from stable carbon isotope analysis. *Journal of Human Evolution* 27:361–72.

Le Vaillant, F. 1790. *Travels from the Cape of Good Hope into the interior parts of Africa*. I. London: William Lane.

Lubbock, J. 1869. *Presentation-historic times as illustrated by ancient remains and the manners and customs of modern savages*. London and Edinburgh: Williams & Norgate.

McBurney, C. B. M. & R. W. Hey. 1955. *Prehistory and Pleistocene geology in Cyrenaican Libya*. Cambridge: Cambridge University Press

McBurney, C. B. M. 1967. *The Haua Fteah (Cyrenaica) and the stone age of the south-east Mediterranean*. Cambridge: Cambridge University Press.

Mandela, N. 1994. *Long walk to freedom*. New York: Little Brown & Co.

Meltzer, L. 1994. Emancipation, commerce and the role of John Fairbairn's Advertiser. In N. Worden & C. Crais (eds), *Breaking the chains: Slavery and its legacy in the nineteenth-century Cape Colony*: 169–99. Johannesburg: Witwatersrand University Press.

Mentzel, O. F. 1944. *A complete and authentic geographical and topographical description of the ... African Cape of Good Hope. (1797)*. H. J. Mandelbrote (rev. & ed.), G. V. Marais & J. Hoge (trans.). Cape Town: Van Riebeeck Society 25.

Mienie, J. H. 1968a. Van Breda, Pieter. *Dictionary of South African Biography* I:810. Cape Town: Nasionale Pers Bpk.

Mienie, J. H. 1968b. Van Breda, Michiel. *Dictionary of South African Biography* I:809–10. Cape Town: Nasionale Pers Bpk.

Norwich, O. I. 1983. Maps of Africa. *An illustrated and annotated carto-bibliography*. Johannesburg: A. D. Donker.

Ondaatje, M. 1992. *The English patient*. New York: Vintage Books.

Pentacost, R. 1992. *Conservation: The farm that died*. Kuils River: Weberprint.

Picard, H. W. J. 1969. *Grand Parade: The birth of greater Cape Town*. Cape Town: C. Struik (Pty) Ltd.

Raven-Hart, R. 1967. *Before Van Riebeeck: Callers at South Africa from 1488 to 1652*. Cape Town: C. Struik (Pty) Ltd.

Schrire, C., J. Deacon, M. Hall & D. Lewis-Williams. 1986. Burkitt's milestone. *Antiquity* 60:123–31.

Schrire, C. 1995. *Digging through darkness: Chronicles of an archaeologist*. Charlottesville: University Press of Virginia.

Shaw, T. 1991. Goodwin's graft, Burkitt's craft. *Antiquity* 65:579–80.

Shell, R. C-H. 1994. *Children of bondage: A social history of the slave society at the Cape of Good Hope 1652–1838*. Hanover and London: Wesleyan University Press.

Smith, A. H. 1978. *Cape views and costumes: Water-colours by H. C. de Meillon in the Brenthurst Collection, Johannesburg*. Johannesburg: The Brenthurst Press.

Sponheimer, M. & J. A. Lee-Thorp. 1999. Isotopic evidence for the diet of an early hominid, *Australopithecus africanus*. *Science* 283:368–70.

Stead, C. J. 1987. *Historical mammal incidence in the Cape Province. 2*. Cape Town: The chief directorate nature and environmental conservation of the provincial administration of the Cape of Good Hope.

Summers, R. F. H. 1975. *A history of the South African Museum 1825–1975*. Cape Town: A. A. Balkema.

Taylor, J. G. 1983. *The social world of Batavia: European and Eurasian in Dutch Asia*. Madison: University of Wisconsin Press.

Thompson, L. 1971. The subjection of the African chiefdoms, 1870–1898, in M. Wilson & L. Thompson (eds), *The Oxford History of South Africa, II, South Africa 1870–1966*: 242–85. Oxford: The Clarendon Press.

Tobias, P. V. 1992. Piltdown: An appraisal of the case against Sir Arthur Keith. *Current Anthropology* 33, 3:243–93.

Tobias, P. V. 1997. Dart, Raymond A(rthur) (1893–1988), in F. Spencer (ed.), *History of physical anthropology, 1 A–L*: 314–15. New York and London: Garland Publishing Inc.

Trollope, A. 1973. *South Africa*. (Reprint of the 1878 edition with an introduction and notes by J. H. Davidson). Cape Town: A. A. Balkema.

Vrba, E. S. 1996. Climate, heterochrony, and human evolutionary theory. *Journal of Anthropological Research* 52: 1–28.

Vergunst, N. 2000. *Hoerikwaggo: Images of Table Mountain*. Cape Town: South African National Gallery.

Wingate, O. 1934. In search of Zezura. *The Geographical Journal* LXXXIII, 4:281–308.

Worden, N. 1994. Between slavery & freedom: The apprenticeship period, 1834–1838. In N. Worden & C. Crais (eds), *Breaking the chains: Slavery and its legacy in the nineteenth-century Cape Colony*: 117–44. Johannesburg: Witwatersrand University Press.

Archival Sources

Cape Archives Depot (CAD):

CSC 2/1/1/6 No 1:17–26. Transcription of Will of Johan Christoffel Muller, 5 June 1816.

CSC 2/1/1/6 No 2:27–35. Transcription of Will of Johan Christoffel Muller, 22 May 1819.

CSC 2/1/1/6 No 3 (a):1–16. Illiquid case in Cape Supreme Court, Martje vs Mabille, qq. 6 March 1829.

CSC 2/1/1/6 No 3 (b):37. A true Extract from the *Cape Town Gazette & African Advertiser* of Saturday, 17 March 1821, Vol. 16, No 192.

MOOC 7/1/84, Doc. Nos 64, 65:599–626. Wills of Johan Christoffel Lodewyk Muller.

SO4/2. Book of Complaint – Guardian of Slaves, 1826–1830.

SO6/13, 14. Register of Slaves, Cape Town and District and Residency of Simonstown.

Illustrations

Cover. A composite of a map of southern Africa, 'Aethiopia inferior vel exterior ... ' by Willem Janszoon Blaeu, Amsterdam, 1635 (Norwich 1983:215). C. Schrire coll., and 'Dexterity of the Hottentots', Author unknown, London, 1795. C. Schrire coll.

1. Bengal tiger cub. Tygerberg Zoo, Cape. Photo C. Schrire.

2. Nelson Mandela and Walter Sisulu, Robben Island, 1966. Photo courtesy University of the Western Cape, Robben Island Museum, Mayibuye Archive.

3. Bengal tiger cub. Tygerberg Zoo, Cape. Photo C. Schrire.

4. Two small moulded polychrome figures of tigers made in China and retrieved from the wreck of the VOC ship, *Oosterland,* wrecked in Table Bay in 1697 (Klose 1994:76 fig. 8). Photo courtesy J. Klose.

5. Lion's Head, Cape Town. Photo C. Schrire.

6. Lion Mountain, Mauritius. The ruins of the VOC Fort, Fredrik Hendrik, lie on the shore in front of the mountain. Photo C. Schrire.

7. 'Vue du Cap de Bonne Esperance.' C. H. du Mal. *c.* 1760. *See* Vergunst, N. 2000:8–9. C. Schrire coll.

8. Animals at the Cape. The tiger is third down on the left (Kolben 1731:131).

9. 'Dangerous Attack of a Tyger.' Le Vaillant 1790: frontispiece. *See* Kennedy 1976, L104.

10. 'Dexterity of the Hottentots'. Newton, delin., Scott sculpt., Artist unknown. I. Wheble, Warwick Court, London, 1 October 1975. C. Schrire coll.

11. 'Vorgebirg der guten Hoffnung.' J. Blaschke. *See* Kennedy 1975, B245. C. Schrire coll.

12. The tiger at the gate of the stockade. Coloured aquatint. Etched by J. Clark after a drawing by Samuel Howett, made from a drawing by Thomas Williamson. Published by Edward Orme, 4 June 1807. *Oriental Field Sports*, plate 12. *See* Archer and Lightbown 1984:67. C. Schrire coll.

13. A tiger hunt. Coloured aquatint, detail. Etched by J. Clark after a drawing by Samuel Howett, made from a drawing by Thomas Williamson. Published by Edward Orme,1 September 1807. *Oriental Field Sports*, plate 17. *See* Archer & Lightbown 1984:67. C. Schrire coll.

14. Tiger, SAM 36950, South African Museum, Cape Town. Photo C. Schrire.

15. The Athenaeum, boyhood home of Glynn Isaac, Newlands, Cape. Photo C. Schrire.

16. View of Cecil John Rhodes' estate on the slopes of Devil's Peak, Cape. Photo C. Schrire.

17. Soapstone bird, Great Zimbabwe. *See* Bent, 1892: facing 151.

18. 'Prospect des Vorgebürges der guten Hoffnung, ...' – 'Vuë du premontoir de bonne Esperance ...' Above in reverse, 'Vuë du premontoir de bonne Esperance.' The mountains are in reverse. G. F. Riedel *c.* 1780. *See* Kennedy 1976, R14; Vergunst 2000:66. Courtesy R. S. Steiger coll.

19. Cape Town. Photo C. Schrire.

20. Castle of Good Hope, Cape Town. T. W. Bowler 1866. *See* Kennedy 1975:B 289. C. Schrire coll.

21. Fort de Goede Hoop at the Cape of Good Hope. O. Dapper 1668. *See* Kennedy 1975, D138; Vergunst 2000: 68–9. C. Schrire coll.

22. 'View in Cape Town: The Barracks.' H. C. de Meillon *c.* 1832–1835. *See* Smith 1978:61. C. Schrire coll.

23. City Hall, Cape Town. Photo C. Schrire.

24. Table Mountain and Table Bay. W. Hodges, 1772. *See* Joppien & Smith 1985:11. *See* Kennedy 1975:H122.

25. Nootka mask, SAM 2361, South African Museum, Cape Town. Photo courtesy of the South African Museum, Cape Town.

26. Chiappini Street, Bo Kaap, Cape Town. Photo C. Schrire.

27. District Six, corner of Caledon and Canterbury Streets. Gregoire Boonzaier, 1964. C. Schrire coll.

28. South African Museum, Cape Town. Photo C. Schrire.

29. *Uranocentrodon,* a large amphibian dating from Middle Beaufort times, *c.* 225 million years ago. South African Museum, Cape Town. Photo C. Schrire.

30. *Erythrosuchus,* a primitive thecodont archosaur of Upper Beaufort times, *c.* 210 million years ago. South African Museum, Cape Town. Photo C. Schrire.

31. The farm Morgenster, Cape. Photo courtesy A. Malan.

32. Mosque, Longmarket Street, Bo Kaap, Cape Town.

Photo C. Schrire.

33. PAGAD (People Against Gangsterism and Drugs) demonstration, Cape Town. *The Times Magazine*, London, 1998:29. Photo courtesy B. Gool.

34. Koopmans-De Wet House, Cape Town. Photo C. Schrire.

35. Interior, Koopmans-De Wet House, Cape Town. Photo C. Schrire.

36. Silver plate candelabrum donated by the Van Breda family, Koopmans-De Wet House, Cape Town. Photo C. Schrire.

37. 'A slave woman and her children,' 1797–1802. Lady Anne Barnard. Photo INIL 7055 (MSB 68). Courtesy of National Library of South Africa, Cape Town.

38. 'View of Cape Town from the Amsterdam Fort.' W. Haines, 1810. *See* Kennedy 1975, H6. C. Schrire coll.

39. 'De Kaap Stad of Tafel Valey.' *c.* 1804. *See* Koopmans-De Wet House 1988:39 No. 261; Vergunst 2000:43. Photo courtesy Pam Warne, South African Cultural History Museum.

40. Michiel van Breda. *See* Burrows, 1952:110.

41. Belfry, *Oranjezicht* homestead, Cape Town. Photo C. Schrire.

42. Bell from Oranjezict, inscribed 'Michiel van Breda 12 Septr 1775.' Koopmans-De Wet House, Cape Town. Photo C. Schrire.

43. 'Our Under-cook.' Lady Anne Barnard 1797–1802. *See* Fairbridge 1924: facing p. 30.

44. 'The Freed Slave.' F. T. I'Ons 1840. MA1961/1234 [188]. *See* Kennedy 1967:176–7. Courtesy of MuseuMAfricA, Newtown, Johannesburg.

45. 'Cap du Bonne Espérance. Vuë de la Montagne de la Table.' J. Milbert 1812. *See* Kennedy 1976, M66. C. Schrire coll.

46. Raymond Dart, shortly after his discovery of the Taung child and his naming it '*Australopithecus africanus*'. *The Star*. *See* Dubow 1995:41.

47. Makapansgat limeworks, Northern Province, South Africa, 1960. Photo C. Schrire.

48. The tiger fight. Coloured aquatint, detail. Etched by J. Clark after a drawing by Samuel Howett, made from a drawing by Thomas Williamson. Published by Edward Orme, 1 August 1807. *Oriental Field Sports*, plate 24. C. Schrire coll.

49. A. J. H. Goodwin *c.* 1930. BC 290. Goodwin Papers. Photo courtesy of Manuscripts and Archives Department, University of Cape Town Libraries.

50. Charles McBurney, far right. Cresswell Crags, 1960. Photo copyright Glynn Isaac, courtesy B. Isaac.

51. Charles McBurney, Cresswell Crags, detail, 1960. Photo copyright Glynn Isaac, courtesy B. Isaac.

52. Count Laslo d'Almàsy records rock art, Libya, 1934. Bermann 1934:468 ff.

53. Glynn (R) as the Original Species and Rhys Isaac (L) as Charles Darwin. Varsity Rag, Cape Town, *c.* 1957. Photo copyright Glynn Isaac, courtesy B. Isaac.

54. The tiger killed by a poisoned arrow. Coloured aquatint, detail. Etched by J. Clark after a drawing by Samuel Howett, made from a drawing by Thomas Williamson. Published by Edward Orme, 1 August 1807. *Oriental Field Sports*, plate 22. C. Schrire coll.

55. The tiger at bay. Coloured aquatint, detail. Etched by J. Clark after a drawing by Samuel Howett, made from a drawing by Thomas Williamson. Published by Edward Orme, 1 August 1807. *Oriental Field Sports*, plate 20. C. Schrire coll.

56. 'Dexterity of the Hottentots'. Artist unknown, London, 1795. C. Schrire coll.

57. Carmel Schrire gives Nelson Mandela a copy of 'Dexterity of the Hottentots' on his 82nd birthday, Johannesburg, 18 July 2000. Photo C. Schrire.

58. Discussing the old issue of tigers in Africa. L to R: Nelson Mandela, Walter Sisulu, Fikile Bam and Carmel Schrire. Johannesburg, 18 July 2000. Photo C. Schrire.

59. The tiger attacks from the sea. Coloured aquatint, detail. Etched by J. Clark after a drawing by Samuel Howett, made from a drawing by Thomas Williamson. Published by Edward Orme, 4 June 1807. *Oriental Field Sports*, plate 36. C. Schrire coll.

60. Tiger. Jules Skøtnes Brown, 2000. C. Schrire coll.